Jazz Phrasing Studies
Volume 1

Universal Edition

by Greg Fishman

GREG FISHMAN
JAZZ STUDIOS

Published by Greg Fishman Jazz Studios
Evanston, Illinois 60202

ISBN: 978-0-9914078-3-5

©2014 Greg Fishman

All rights reserved. International copyright secured. No part of this book or CD set may be reproduced or transmitted in any form or by any means, electronic or mechanical, including photocopying or recording, or by any information storage and retrieval system, without permission in writing from the publisher. Violation of copyright is subject to all applicable laws.

Published by Greg Fishman Jazz Studios
824 Custer Avenue, Evanston, Illinois 60202 U.S.A.
www.gregfishmanjazzstudios.com

Jazz Phrasing Studies Volume 1

Universal Edition

Table of Contents

Preface 4
Credits 5
Suggested Use of This Book and CD Set 6
Style and Analysis 9
Style and Analysis 11

Song Title	Treble Clef	Bb	Eb	Bass Clef
Milwaukee Avenue	12	34	56	78
Ogden Avenue	14	36	58	80
Narragansett Avenue	16	38	60	82
Belden Avenue	18	40	62	84
Chicago Avenue	20	42	64	86
Quincy Street	22	44	66	88
Rockwell Street	24	46	68	90
Dearborn Street	26	48	70	92
Franklin Street	28	50	72	94
Pearson Street	30	52	74	96

About the Author 104

©2014 Greg Fishman
All rights reserved. International copyright secured.

PREFACE

Applying good phrasing to music is like using good punctuation in written or spoken language. It involves the grouping of ideas to make the meaning of the words clear to the listener. The words are grouped into sentences, and the sentences are then grouped into paragraphs. The same is true when interpreting a piece of music.

Good phrasing requires a musician to interpret the notes he plays, and determine which notes need to be grouped together to form a complete musical idea. Throughout this book, each song is designed to train your ear to hear the logical grouping of phrases through the use of sequence and thematic development.

While the art of good phrasing involves the interpretation of note groupings and their relationships, it also involves deciding where you're going to take a breath.

Read the following sentences aloud to compare examples of good and bad phrasing.

<u>Good phrasing, spoken in one continuous breath:</u>

"Ladies and gentlemen, it gives me great pleasure to introduce the senior class president."

<u>Bad phrasing, spoken with extra breaths, disrupting the flow and grouping of the words:</u>

"Ladies and gentlemen, it gives (breath) me great pleasure to introduce the senior class (breath) president."

The difference between these two sentences is very similar to the difference between a professional musician's phrasing and a student's phrasing. Both may be playing the correct notes with the correct rhythm, but the professional musician knows how to group the notes in a smooth, flowing fashion, while the student takes breaths at random, not even aware that he's disrupting the phrasing.

Jazz Phrasing for Saxophone has been carefully designed to help you learn to phrase like a professional player.

These are pieces that will be fun for all musicians who love melodic writing with good thematic development. I hope that you get many years of enjoyment from this book.

— Greg Fishman

CREDITS

Published by Greg Fishman Jazz Studios, Evanston, Illinois
Edited by: Judy Roberts
Cover photo: New Trier High School Jazz Ensemble
Graphic design: Russ Paladino
Music engraving: Greg Fishman
Consultant: Nic Meyer

CD Recorded at Studiomedia, Evanston, Illinois
Engineered, mixed and mastered by Scott Steinman

Greg Fishman – Alto & Tenor Saxophone
Victor Garcia – Trumpet
Russ Phillips – Trombone
Dennis Luxion – Piano
Eric Hochberg – Bass
Phil Gratteau – Drums

Greg Fishman is a D'Addario Woodwind artist and plays Rico reeds exclusively.

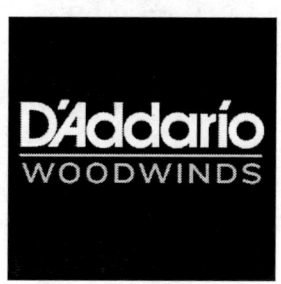

SUGGESTED USE OF THIS BOOK AND CD SET

USING THE PLAY-ALONG CD

The play-along CD contains twenty-one tracks. The odd-numbered tracks feature a demonstration version of each song. The even-numbered CD tracks feature the rhythm section only. (Track 21 features tuning notes of concert "A" and "Bb.")

If you'd like to play along with the demonstration track and then immediately play the same piece again with the rhythm section, simply play through the entire CD, track by track.

To play through the entire book using only the demonstration tracks, simply program your CD player to play the odd-numbered tracks only (1,3,5,7, etc.).

To play through the entire book with just the rhythm section tracks, program your CD player to play the even-numbered tracks only (2,4,6,8, etc.).

The demonstration tracks should be used to get the general feel and mood of each piece. When playing along, try to match the phrasing, time-feel and articulation used by the soloist on the recording.

The rhythm section tracks are great for practicing the melody, arpeggiating the chords, scales, voice-leading lines, etc.

Once you're comfortable playing along with the recorded demonstration and rhythm section tracks, improvise a solo over the play-along tracks. This is a fun way to explore the music and a great way to train your ear.

TEMPOS

The pieces in this book focus primarily on medium tempos. However, if you feel that you can't yet keep up with the recorded tempo, set your metronome below the marked tempo and play through the piece. Circle any passage that poses a technical challenge, and practice the circled areas until you can play them smoothly and accurately. The final "test" for any tempo is whether or not you can successfully play the entire piece in time, with the correct style and articulation, with no mistakes. Once you've achieved this goal, you're ready to turn the metronome one click faster. Continue repeating this process until you've reached the marked tempo.

DYNAMICS

A suggested dynamic level is marked at the beginning of each song. However, within each piece, and each phrase, there are often what I call "micro-dynamics." These are subtle differences between the weighting of notes in a phrase, and they have a dramatic effect on the phrasing and feel of the piece. If you listen carefully to the recording, you can hear the performer making these dynamic choices, too subtle and numerous to notate, but there for you to hear and study, nonetheless.

Think of these micro-dynamics as you would think of small waves of water on a smooth lake. The lake is calm, but there's still some movement in the water, as opposed to a pail of water with no motion whatsoever.

I encourage you to experiment with different dynamics on the pieces, and, as a general rule, start the pieces at a comfortably moderate dynamic level so that you leave yourself some room to build the dynamic level for the repeat of the piece.

ARTICULATION

Crisp, clear articulation in music is the equivalent of good diction used in any spoken language. Throughout this book I have included articulation markings to convey the basic style of each piece. However, I recommend repeated listenings to the play-along CDs, which will reveal more subtle nuances of articulation.

VOICE-LEADING

Voice-leading is the smooth connection (moving a distance of not more than a whole-step) from a note in one chord, to a note in the next chord. Voice-leading gives a polished, sophisticated quality to a phrase.

For an example of effective voice-leading, look at the concert key version of *Narragansett Avenue.* Notice that the "Eb" (the seventh of Fmi7) on beat three of the first measure resolves to the "D" (the third of Bb7) on the upbeat of beat four, and ties into the "D" in the second measure. This is the essence of good voice-leading, because it highlights the sound of the current chord changing to a new chord with a minimum of movement.

In the situation described above, the voice-leading is descending, but it is important to note that voice-leading can also ascend. In the concert key version of *Pearson Street,* the "Db" on beat three (the root of Db9) in the twenty-sixth measure resolves upwards by a half-step to the "D" (the fifth of Gmi7) in measure twenty-seven.

When studying the pieces in this book, always take note of the voice-leading used in the construction of the phrases.

USING THIS BOOK WITH AN ENSEMBLE

This book is a great resource for band directors to use with the jazz ensemble. These songs will serve as perfect vehicles for daily warm-ups. They're excellent for working on sight-reading, intonation, phrasing, articulation, section balance, blending, etc.

Band directors can easily create instant arrangements by using the rehearsal letters on each song to assign parts to different sections of the band. For example, the saxophone section could play at letter "A," the trumpets at letter "B," trombones at letter "C," and with the full ensemble at letter "D." Soloists can then be featured playing over the form of the song. Portions of the written melody can also be used as backgrounds for the soloist.

Another approach would be to combine different instruments from each section of the band to play the melody. For example, altos and trumpets could play at letter "A," with tenors and trombones playing at letter "B." Letter "C" could be used as an eight-measure solo, and the full ensemble can come in at letter "D."

Band directors are also encouraged to experiment with many different combinations of instruments to address their particular ensemble needs. For example, sometimes trumpet and tenor may need to work on matching their tonal blend and intonation. To achieve this goal, the band director might have the full ensemble play at letters "A" and "B" and have only the trumpet and tenor play in unison at letter "C."

This book can also be used for ear-training purposes. One of the best ways to improve the ear is to hear the relationship of the melody notes to the roots of the chords. For example, the trombone section can play the root of each chord, while the saxophone section plays the melody. On the repeat of the song, the saxes can play the roots, while the trumpets and trombones play the melody.

The roots of the chords are easy for everyone to play, because the letter name is part of the chord. However, the remaining notes in the chords (3rds, 5ths, 7ths, etc.) are often a mystery to aspiring players. If the band director wants to work on chord spellings with the full ensemble, he could go through a song multiple times, with the group playing a specific chord tone throughout the form.

For example, the first time through the song, the ensemble can play the roots of the chords. The second time through, they can play the thirds. The third time through, they can play the fifths, then the sevenths, etc. This approach will quickly reveal any shortcomings in the student's knowledge of chord spellings, allowing these issues to be addressed and improved in a fun, interactive way.

MORE RESOURCES AVAILABLE ONLINE

If you'd like to read more about my concepts on jazz improvisation, please visit my educational website: www.gregfishmanjazzstudios.com.

STYLE & ANALYSIS

SEQUENCES

Sequences make a song sound more structured and melodic. They involve the use of repeated melodic, rhythmic or harmonic patterns. The pitches of the repeated pattern are often transposed to fit a new harmonic setting.

Sequences usually occur in groups of two or three, with the original idea serving as the "model" sequence upon which subsequent sequences are based. The challenge for a composer or improvisor using sequences is knowing how many times to repeat an idea. If there are too few sequences, the song won't sound catchy, yet, if you have too many sequences, the song gets too predictable. When you have the right number of sequences, a song sounds melodically balanced.

Play through the following example and notice the way in which sequence is used to give the song a "catchy" sound:

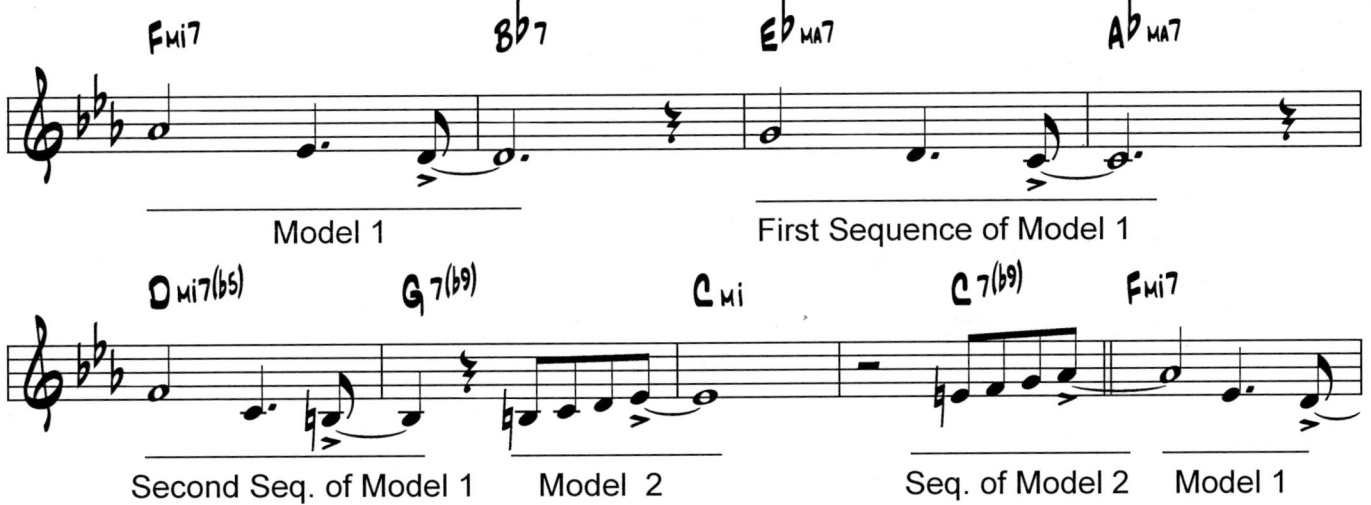

"Narragansett Avenue," mm.1-9

In the example above, the opening theme is sequenced twice, for a total of three statements of the melodic idea. In the sixth measure of the example, a new idea is introduced, which is then sequenced in the eighth measure, which leads back to a restatement of the "Model 1" idea. The final note in the sequence of "Model 2" (the upbeat of beat four, measure eight) is tied to the first note of the restatement of "Model 1." This "sharing" of the last note of "Model 2" and the first note of "Model 1" links the two ideas smoothly together.

As an experiment to demonstrate the importance and power of sequence, play the example above, and put rests in the fifth measure in place of the notes. Your ear will hear that the "Model 1" idea hasn't been repeated enough times, and you'll feel as though the musical thought stopped in mid-sentence.

Next, play the excerpt above once more, but as originally written, without the rests in the fifth measure. When you hear the third statement of the theme in the fifth measure, you'll hear that the phrase is now balanced and complete. If you want to hear some truly amazing sequences, listen to any music by J.S. Bach, one of my all-time musical heroes.

VARIATIONS ON A THEME

While sequence is used to restate a theme, often transposing the idea to fit into a new harmonic context, variation is used to elaborate on the theme by changing some of the rhythms, sometimes adding new notes in the middle of the theme, or by changing the ending of the theme.

Play through the variations used in "Franklin Street" below:

"Franklin Street," mm.1-3

"Franklin Street," mm.9-11

"Franklin Street," mm.17-19

"Franklin Street," mm.25-27

The example above contains three variations on the original theme used in "Franklin Street." Notice the way in which the original idea has evolved. Carefully compare each variation and notice what has changed from the original version of the theme. This type of analysis is quite valuable, as you'll want to develop the ability to use the theme and variation concept in your own improvisations.

SUGGESTIONS FOR FURTHER ANALYSIS

As you get familiar with the ten pieces in this book, make a mental note of the phrases which are your favorites. Try to analyze what you like about the phrase. If you can figure out *why* you like it, and determine the musical construction of the idea, you'll be able to take the concept and incorporate it into your own playing and writing.

DETAILED OVERVIEW OF THE SONGS

Title	Tempo	Form	Length of Form	Key Signature (Concert)	Demo Track Instrument	CD Track Numbers
Milwaukee Avenue	♩= 108	BLUES	12 Bars	Eb Major	Alto Sax	1. & 2.
Ogden Avenue	♩= 144	AABA	32 Bars	F Major	Trumpet	3. & 4.
Narragansett Avenue	♩= 126	AABC	32 Bars	C Minor	Tenor Sax	5. & 6.
Belden Avenue	♩= 138	AABA	56 Bars	C Major	Trombone	7. & 8.
Chicago Avenue	♩= 132	AABA	32 Bars	F Major	Tenor Sax	9. & 10.
Quincy Street	♩= 152	AABA	32 Bars	Eb Major	Alto Sax	11. & 12.
Rockwell Street	♩= 144	AABA	32 Bars	G Minor	Trumpet	13. & 14.
Dearborn Street	♩= 160	ABAB	32 Bars	C Major	Trombone	15. & 16.
Franklin Street	♩= 112	ABAC	32 Bars	D Minor	Trumpet	17. & 18.
Pearson Street	♩= 144	ABAC	36 Bars	Eb Major	Alto Sax	19. & 20.

CD TRACK #1 (DEMONSTRATION TRACK)
CD TRACK #2 (RHYTHM SECTION ONLY)
COUNT OFF: 2 BARS (6 CLICKS)

GREG FISHMAN

Milwaukee Avenue

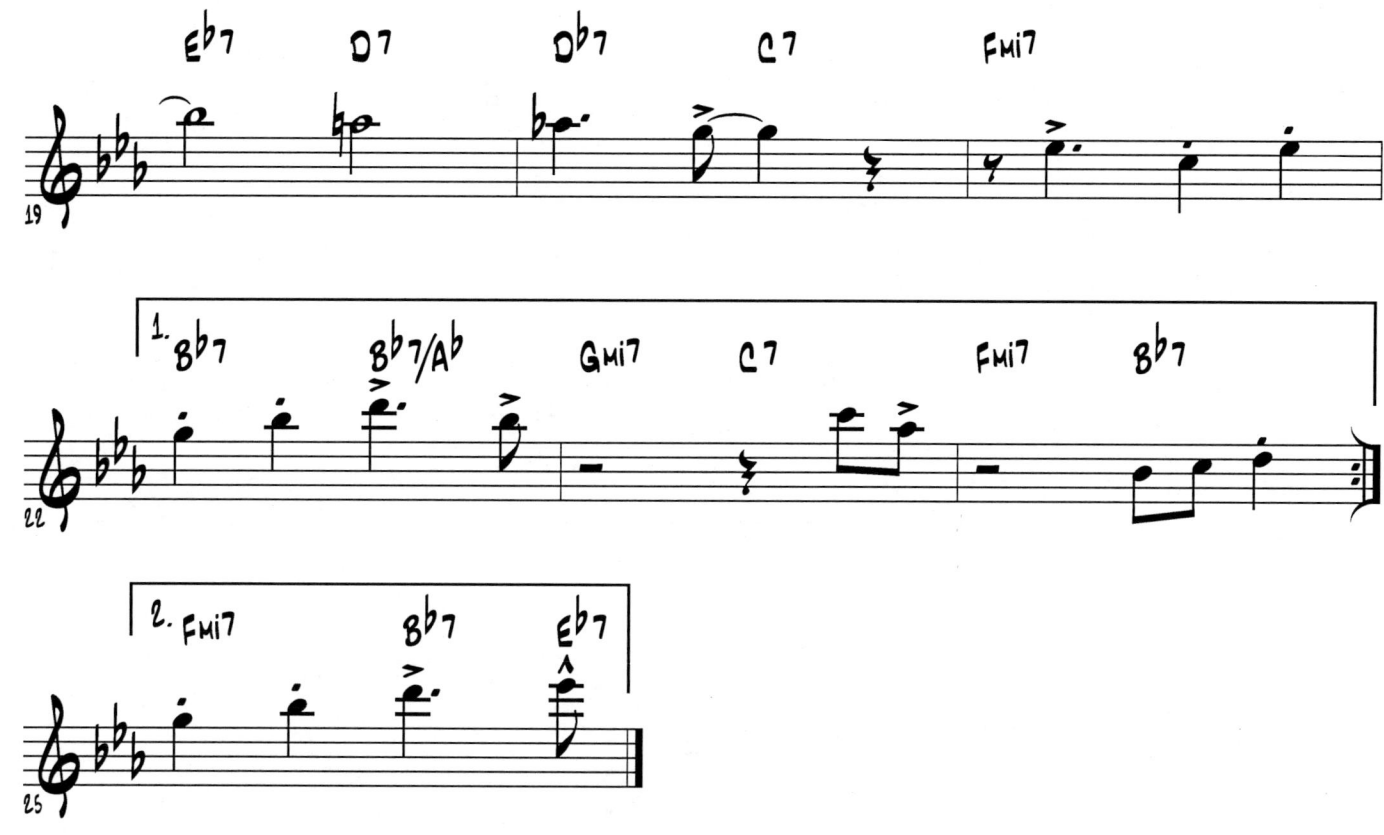

CD TRACK #3 (DEMONSTRATION TRACK)
CD TRACK #4 (RHYTHM SECTION ONLY)
COUNT OFF: 2 BARS (6 CLICKS)

GREG FISHMAN

Ogden Avenue

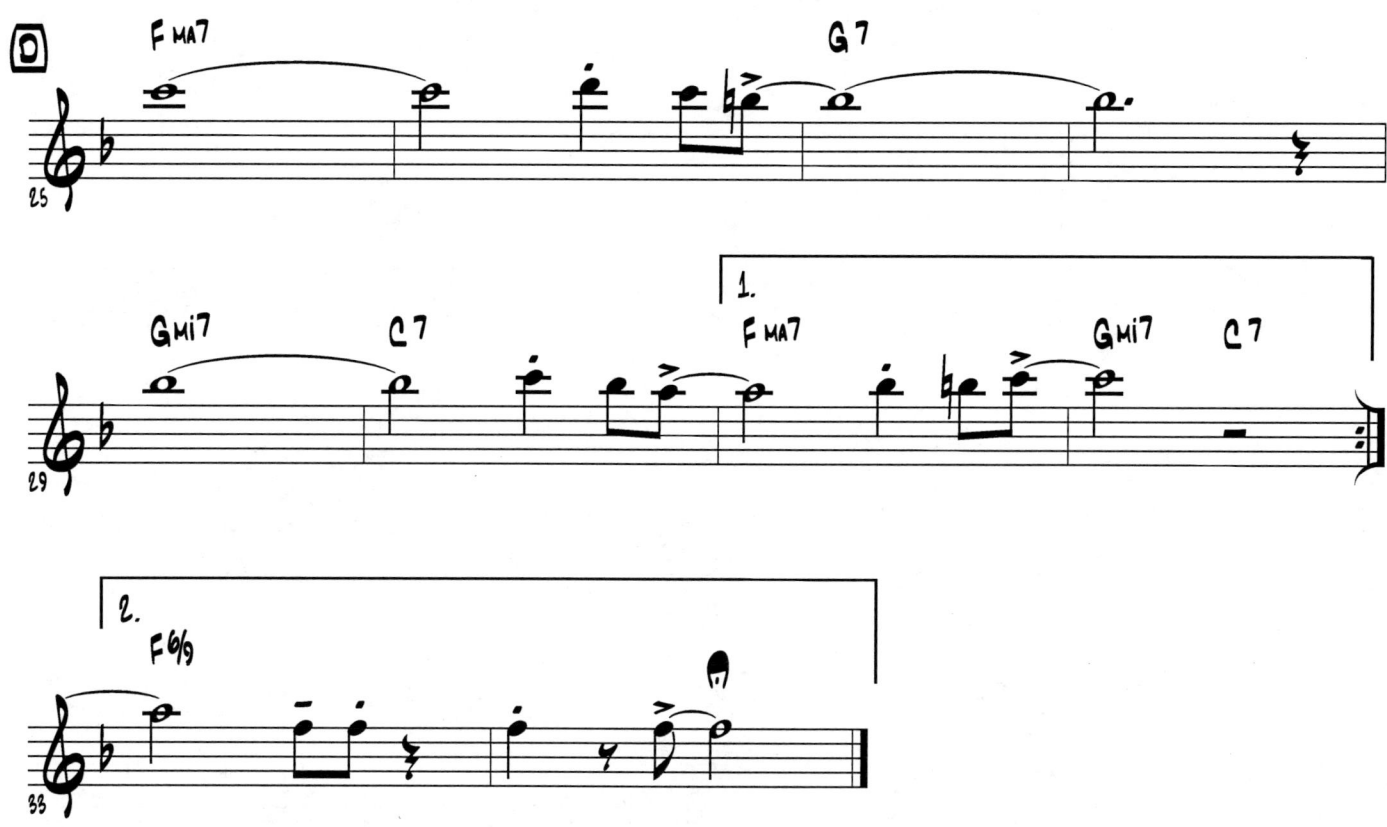

CD TRACK #5 (DEMONSTRATION TRACK)
CD TRACK #6 (RHYTHM SECTION ONLY)

COUNT OFF: 2 BARS (6 CLICKS)

Greg Fishman

Narragansett Avenue

CD TRACK #9 (DEMONSTRATION TRACK)
CD TRACK #10 (RHYTHM SECTION ONLY)
COUNT OFF: 2 BARS (6 CLICKS)

GREG FISHMAN

Chicago Avenue

CD TRACK #11 (DEMONSTRATION TRACK)
CD TRACK #12 (RHYTHM SECTION ONLY)
COUNT OFF: 2 BARS (6 CLICKS)

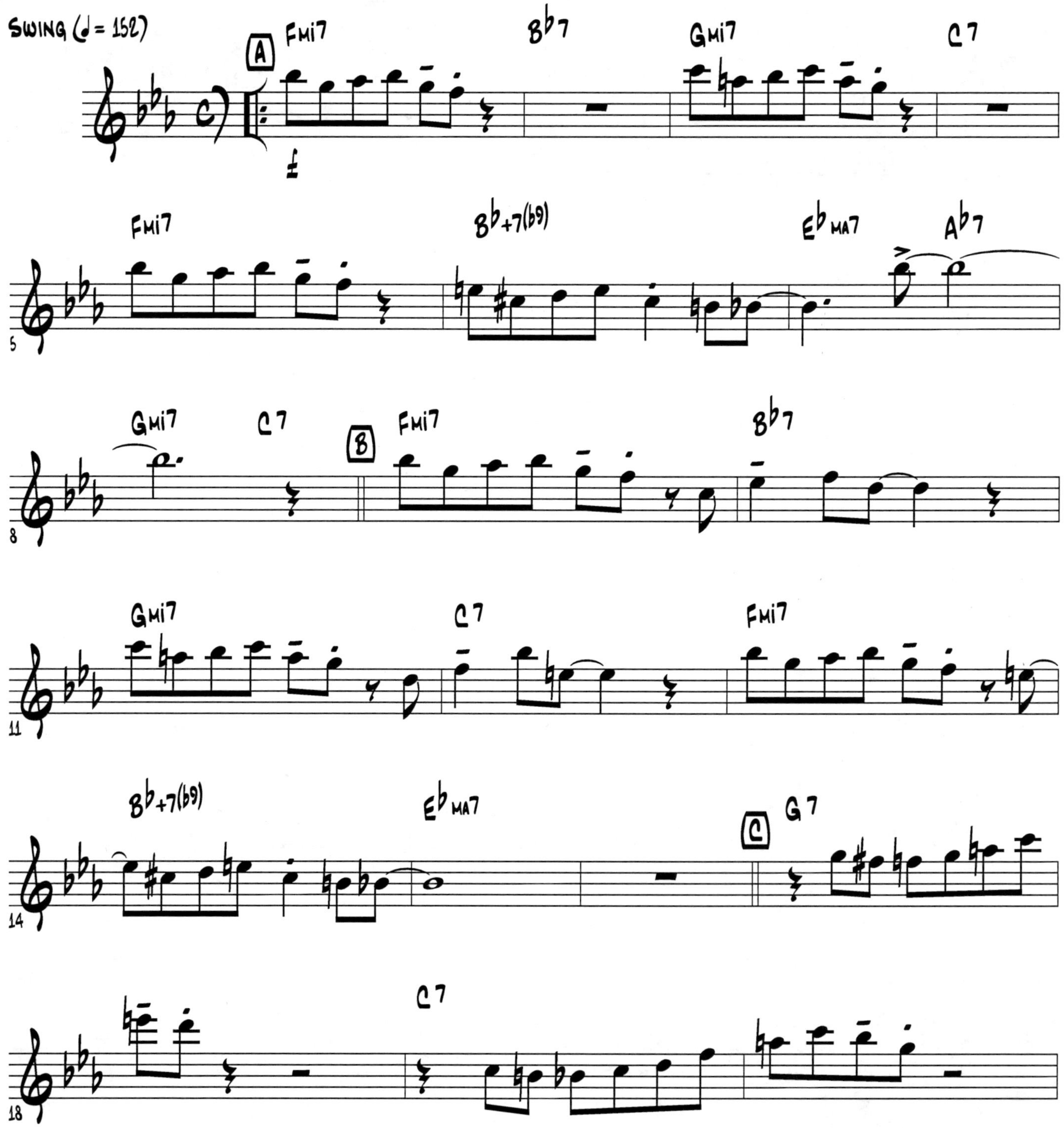

GREG FISHMAN

Quincy Street

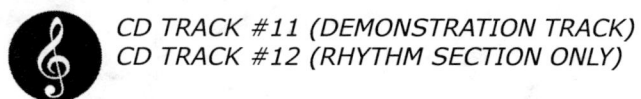

CD TRACK #13 (DEMONSTRATION TRACK)
CD TRACK #14 (RHYTHM SECTION ONLY)

COUNT OFF: 2 BARS (6 CLICKS)

GREG FISHMAN

Rockwell Street

CD TRACK #15 (DEMONSTRATION TRACK)
CD TRACK #16 (RHYTHM SECTION ONLY)
COUNT OFF: 2 BARS (6 CLICKS)

Greg Fishman

Dearborn Street

(Optional 8vb)

©2014 Greg Fishman Jazz Studios
All Rights Reserved. Copyright Secured.

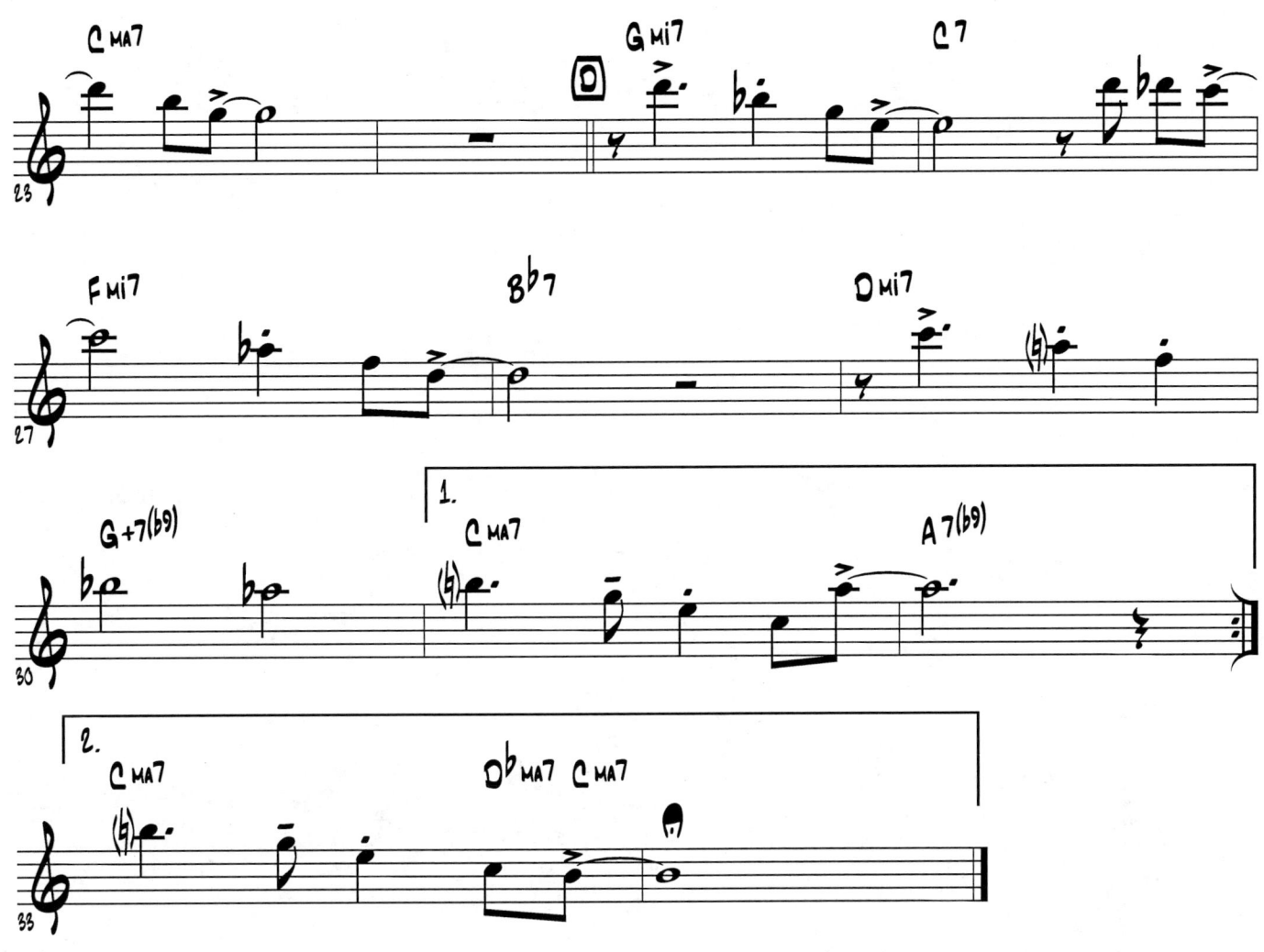

CD TRACK #17 (DEMONSTRATION TRACK)
CD TRACK #18 (RHYTHM SECTION ONLY)
COUNT OFF: 2 BARS (6 CLICKS)

Greg Fishman

Franklin Street

CD TRACK #19 (DEMONSTRATION TRACK)
CD TRACK #20 (RHYTHM SECTION ONLY)
COUNT OFF: 2 BARS (6 CLICKS)

Greg Fishman

Pearson Street

(Optional 8vb)

Jazz Phrasing Studies
Volume 1

Table of Contents - Bb Instruments

Milwaukee Avenue	34
Ogden Avenue	36
Narragansett Avenue	38
Belden Avenue	40
Chicago Avenue	42
Quincy Street	44
Rockwell Street	46
Dearborn Street	48
Franklin Street	50
Pearson Street	52

©2014 Greg Fishman
All rights reserved. International copyright secured.

Bb — CD TRACK #3 (DEMONSTRATION TRACK)
CD TRACK #4 (RHYTHM SECTION ONLY)
COUNT OFF: 2 BARS (6 CLICKS)

Greg Fishman

Ogden Avenue

(Tenor Saxophone - Optional 8va)

©2014 Greg Fishman Jazz Studios
All Rights Reserved. Copyright Secured.

Bb

CD TRACK #5 (DEMONSTRATION TRACK)
CD TRACK #6 (RHYTHM SECTION ONLY)

Greg Fishman

COUNT OFF: 2 BARS (6 CLICKS)

Narragansett Avenue

(Tenor Saxophone - Optional 8va*)

*Note: If Tenor Sax is playing in the lower register, play the note in the parenthesis for measure 19.

Bb

CD TRACK #9 (DEMONSTRATION TRACK)
CD TRACK #10 (RHYTHM SECTION ONLY)
COUNT OFF: 2 BARS (6 CLICKS)

GREG FISHMAN

Chicago Avenue

42

B♭

CD TRACK #11 (DEMONSTRATION TRACK)
CD TRACK #12 (RHYTHM SECTION ONLY)
COUNT OFF: 2 BARS (6 CLICKS)

Greg Fishman

Quincy Street

(Tenor Saxophone - Optional 8va)

44

45

CD TRACK #13 (DEMONSTRATION TRACK)
CD TRACK #14 (RHYTHM SECTION ONLY)

COUNT OFF: 2 BARS (6 CLICKS)

Greg Fishman

Rockwell Street

(Tenor Saxophone - Optional 8va)

Swing ($\quarternote = 144$)

©2014 Greg Fishman Jazz Studios
All Rights Reserved. Copyright Secured.

Bb — CD TRACK #15 (DEMONSTRATION TRACK)
CD TRACK #16 (RHYTHM SECTION ONLY)
COUNT OFF: 2 BARS (6 CLICKS)

Greg Fishman

Dearborn Street

Bb — CD TRACK #17 (DEMONSTRATION TRACK)
CD TRACK #18 (RHYTHM SECTION ONLY)
COUNT OFF: 2 BARS (6 CLICKS)

Greg Fishman

Franklin Street

(Tenor Saxophone - Optional 8va)

Bb

CD TRACK #19 (DEMONSTRATION TRACK)
CD TRACK #20 (RHYTHM SECTION ONLY)

COUNT OFF: 2 BARS (6 CLICKS)

Greg Fishman

Pearson Street

(Tenor Saxophone - Optional 8va*)

*Note: If Tenor Sax is playing in the lower register, play the note in the parenthesis for measure 18.

Jazz Phrasing Studies
Volume 1

Table of Contents - Eb Instruments

Milwaukee Avenue	56
Ogden Avenue	58
Narragansett Avenue	60
Belden Avenue	62
Chicago Avenue	64
Quincy Street	66
Rockwell Street	68
Dearborn Street	70
Franklin Street	72
Pearson Street	74

©2014 Greg Fishman
All rights reserved. International copyright secured.

Eb

CD TRACK #1 (DEMONSTRATION TRACK)
CD TRACK #2 (RHYTHM SECTION ONLY)

COUNT OFF: 2 BARS (6 CLICKS)

GREG FISHMAN

Milwaukee Avenue

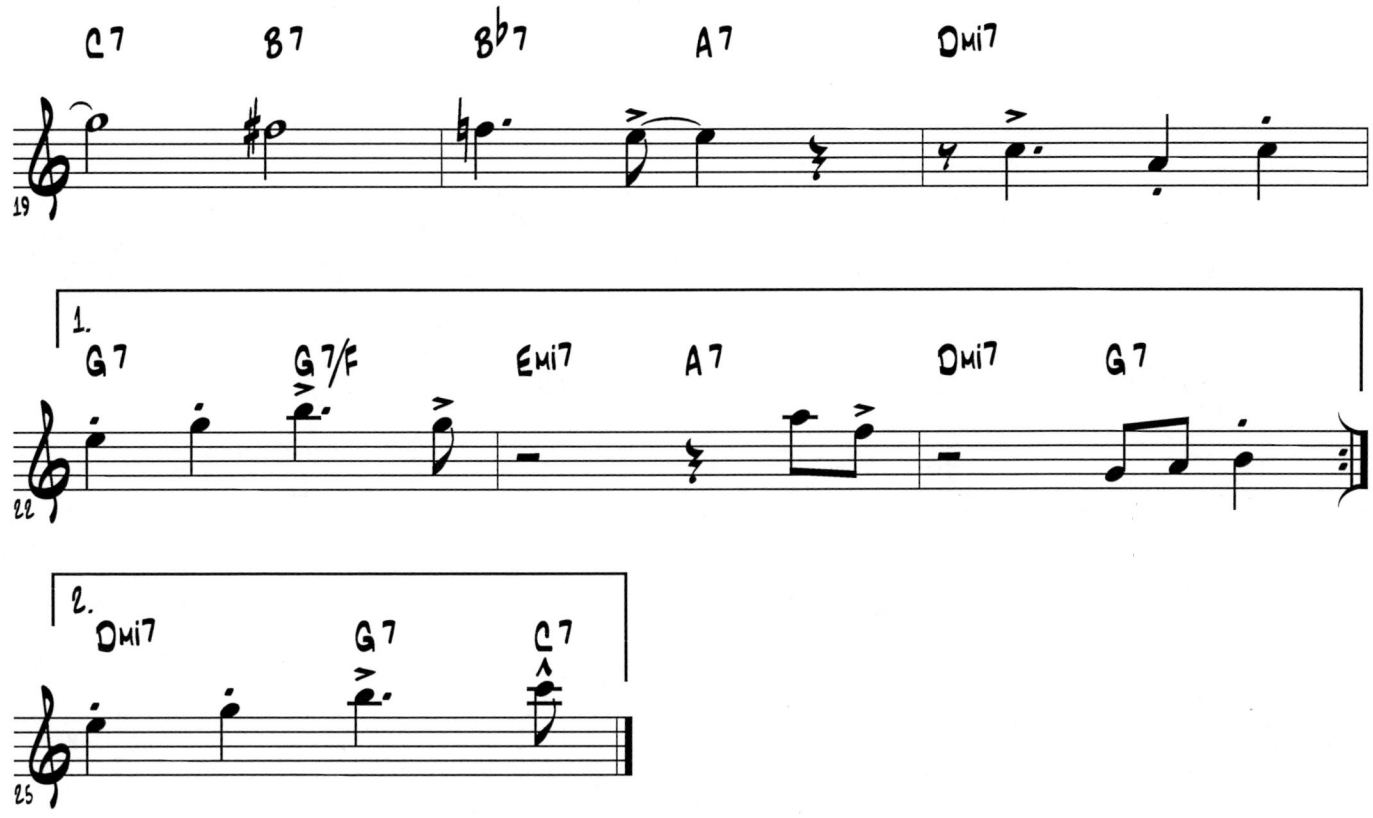

CD TRACK #3 (DEMONSTRATION TRACK)
CD TRACK #4 (RHYTHM SECTION ONLY)

COUNT OFF: 2 BARS (6 CLICKS)

Greg Fishman

Ogden Avenue

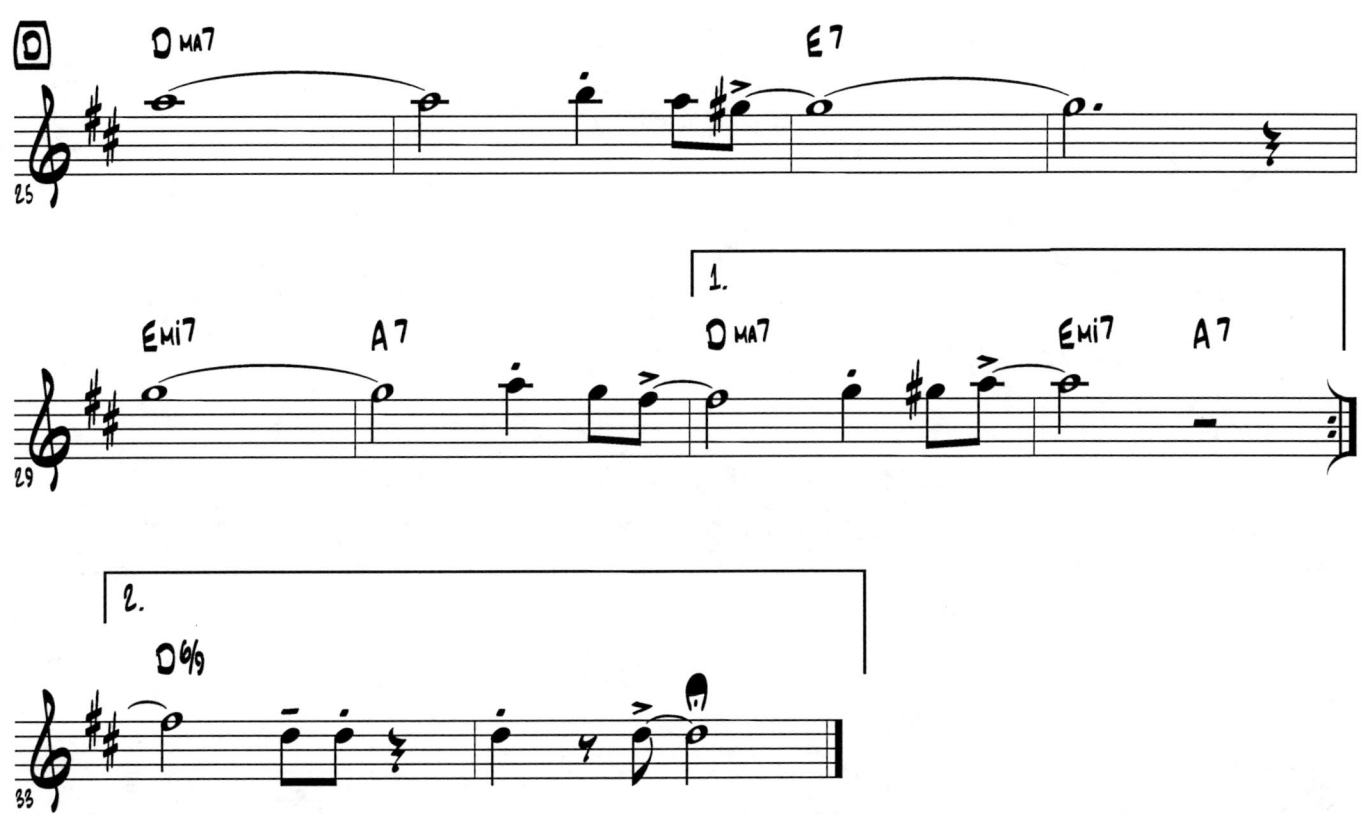

CD TRACK #5 (DEMONSTRATION TRACK)
CD TRACK #6 (RHYTHM SECTION ONLY)

COUNT OFF: 2 BARS (6 CLICKS)

Greg Fishman

Narragansett Avenue

60

Eb

CD TRACK #9 (DEMONSTRATION TRACK)
CD TRACK #10 (RHYTHM SECTION ONLY)
COUNT OFF: 2 BARS (6 CLICKS)

GREG FISHMAN

Chicago Avenue

Eb

CD TRACK #11 (SAXOPHONE + RHYTHM SECTION)
CD TRACK #12 (RHYTHM SECTION ONLY)

COUNT OFF: 2 BARS (6 CLICKS)

GREG FISHMAN

QUINCY STREET

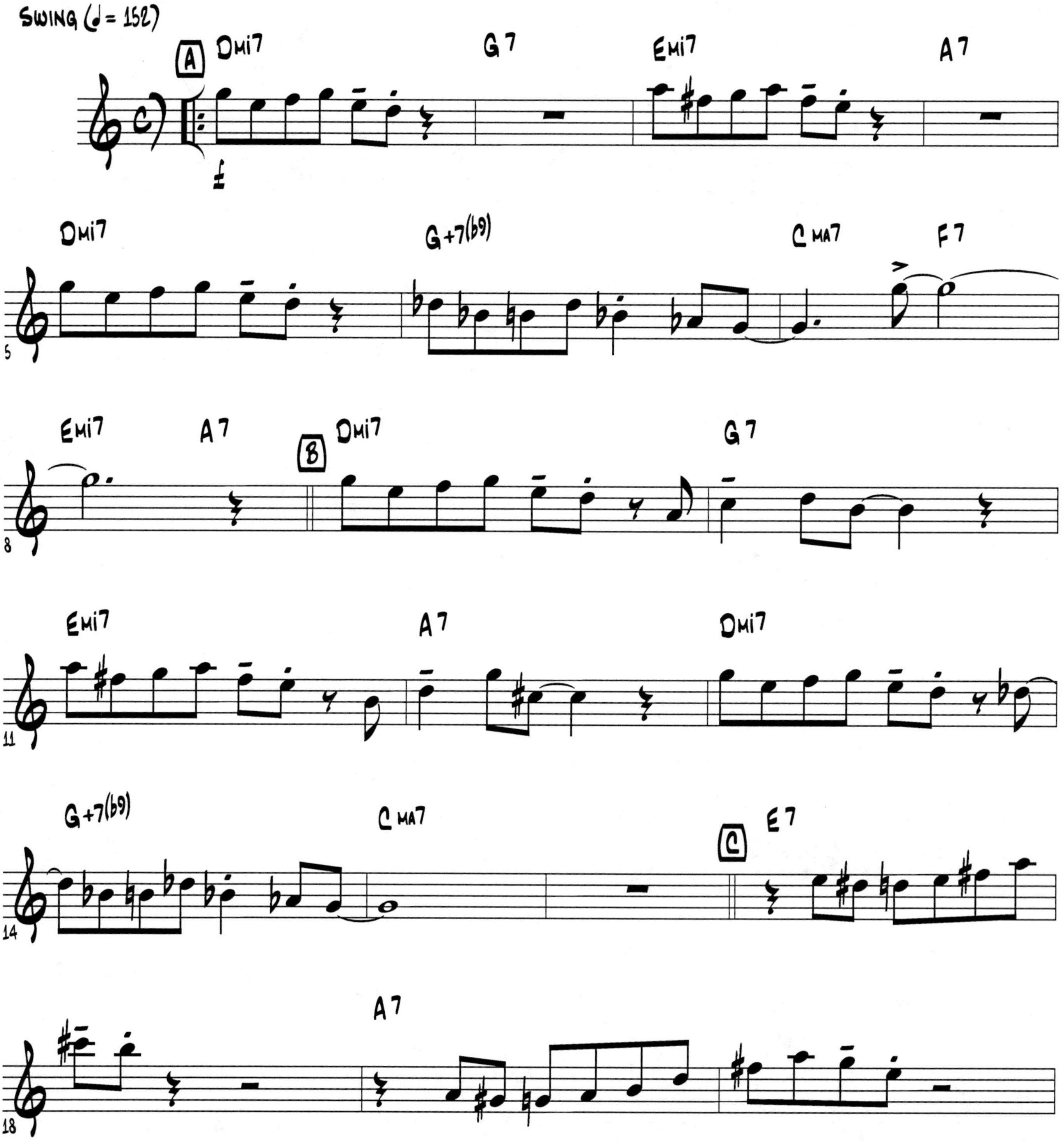

E♭

CD TRACK #13 (DEMONSTRATION TRACK)
CD TRACK #14 (RHYTHM SECTION ONLY)

COUNT OFF: 2 BARS (6 CLICKS)

GREG FISHMAN

Rockwell Street

68
©2014 Greg Fishman Jazz Studios
All Rights Reserved. Copyright Secured.

CD TRACK #15 (DEMONSTRATION TRACK)
CD TRACK #16 (RHYTHM SECTION ONLY)

COUNT OFF: 2 BARS (6 CLICKS)

Greg Fishman

Dearborn Street

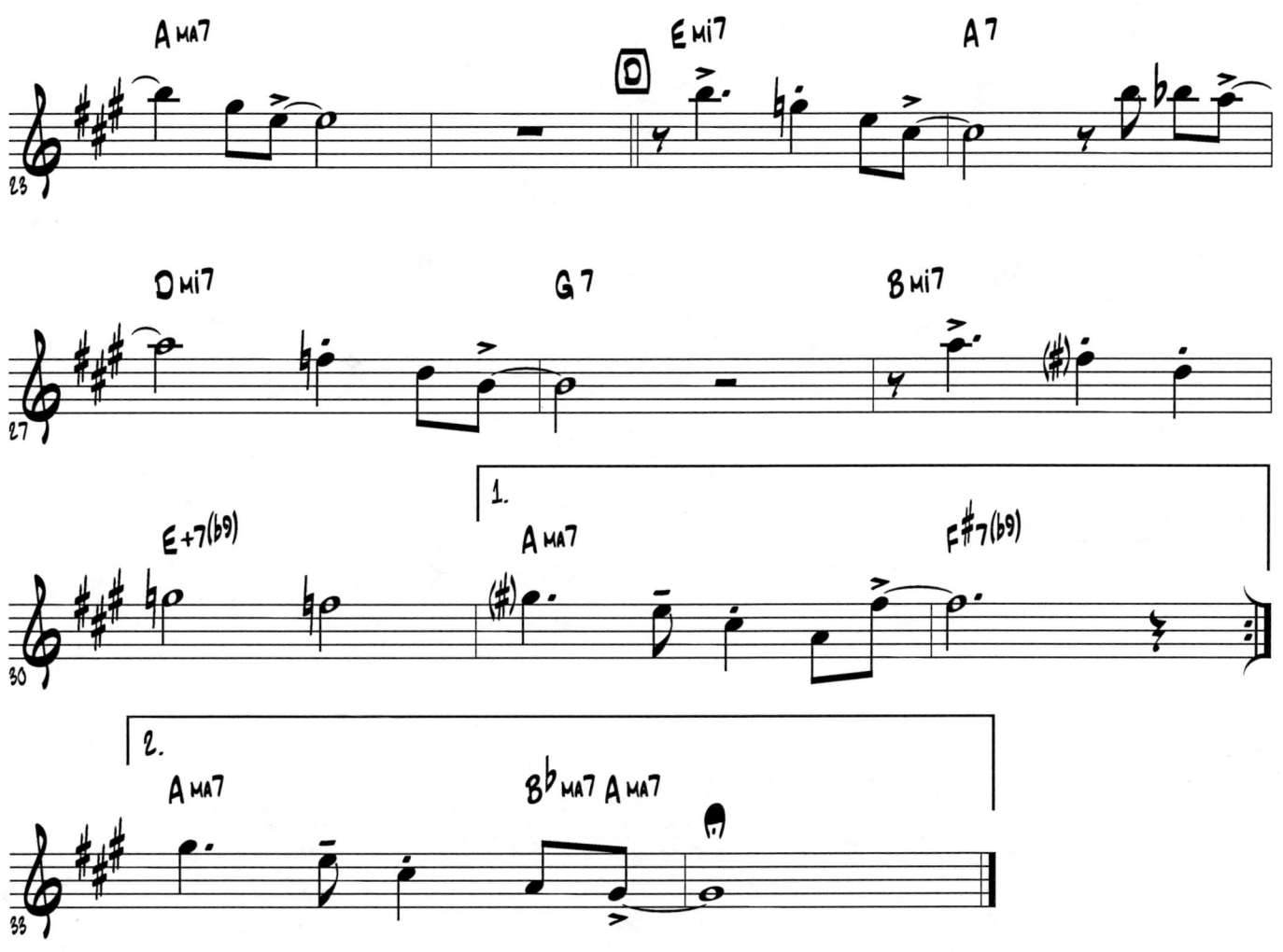

E♭

CD TRACK #17 (DEMONSTRATION TRACK)
CD TRACK #18 (RHYTHM SECTION ONLY)

COUNT OFF: 2 BARS (6 CLICKS)

GREG FISHMAN

Franklin Street

72

Jazz Phrasing Studies Volume 1

Table of Contents - Bass Clef Instruments

Milwaukee Avenue	78
Ogden Avenue	80
Narragansett Avenue	82
Belden Avenue	84
Chicago Avenue	86
Quincy Street	88
Rockwell Street	90
Dearborn Street	92
Franklin Street	94
Pearson Street	96

©2014 Greg Fishman
All rights reserved. International copyright secured.

CD TRACK #1 (DEMONSTRATION TRACK)
CD TRACK #2 (RHYTHM SECTION ONLY)
COUNT OFF: 2 BARS (6 CLICKS)

GREG FISHMAN

Milwaukee Avenue

CD TRACK #3 (DEMONSTRATION TRACK)
CD TRACK #4 (RHYTHM SECTION ONLY)

COUNT OFF: 2 BARS (6 CLICKS)

Greg Fishman

Ogden Avenue

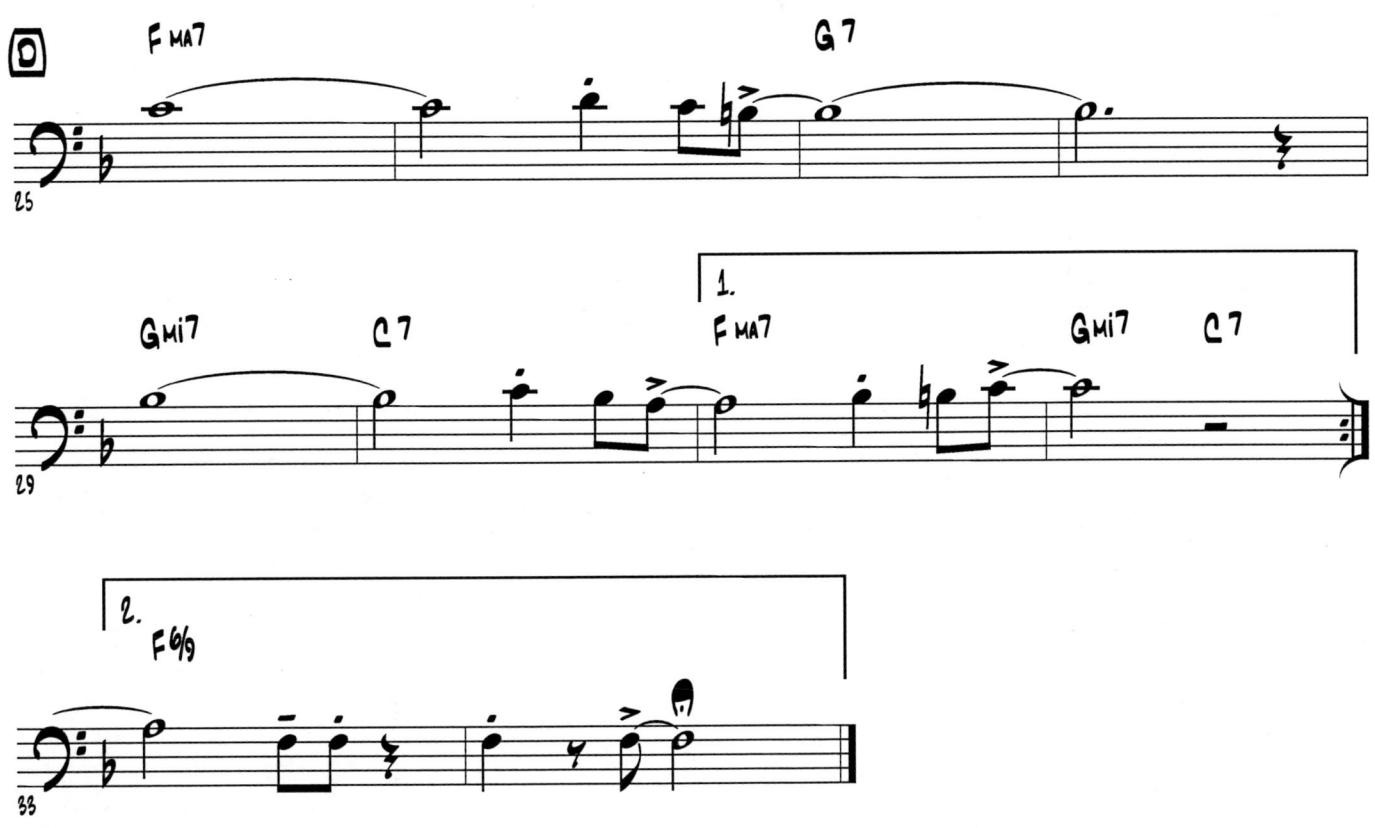

CD TRACK #5 (DEMONSTRATION TRACK)
CD TRACK #6 (RHYTHM SECTION ONLY)

COUNT OFF: 2 BARS (6 CLICKS)

GREG FISHMAN

Narragansett Avenue

CD TRACK #7 (DEMONSTRATION TRACK)
CD TRACK #8 (RHYTHM SECTION ONLY)

GREG FISHMAN

COUNT OFF: 2 BARS (6 CLICKS)

Belden Avenue

Bossa Nova (♩ = 138)

CD TRACK #9 (DEMONSTRATION TRACK)
CD TRACK #10 (RHYTHM SECTION ONLY)

COUNT OFF: 2 BARS (6 CLICKS)

GREG FISHMAN

Chicago Avenue

CD TRACK #11 (DEMONSTRATION TRACK)
CD TRACK #12 (RHYTHM SECTION ONLY)

COUNT OFF: 2 BARS (6 CLICKS)

Greg Fishman

Quincy Street

CD TRACK #13 (DEMONSTRATION TRACK)
CD TRACK #14 (RHYTHM SECTION ONLY)

COUNT OFF: 2 BARS (6 CLICKS)

Rockwell Street

Greg Fishman

CD TRACK #15 (DEMONSTRATION TRACK)
CD TRACK #16 (RHYTHM SECTION ONLY)

COUNT OFF: 2 BARS (6 CLICKS)

Greg Fishman

Dearborn Street

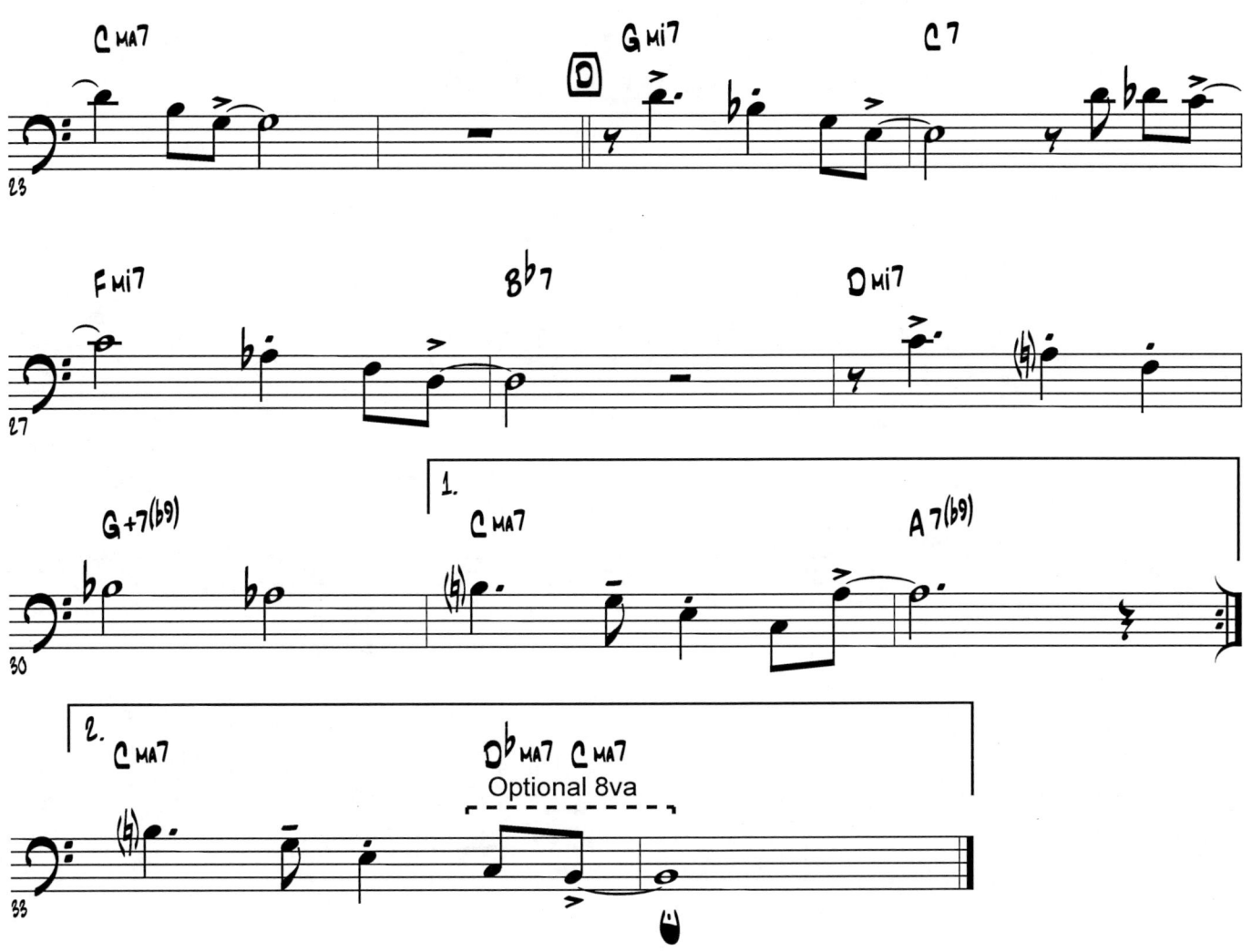

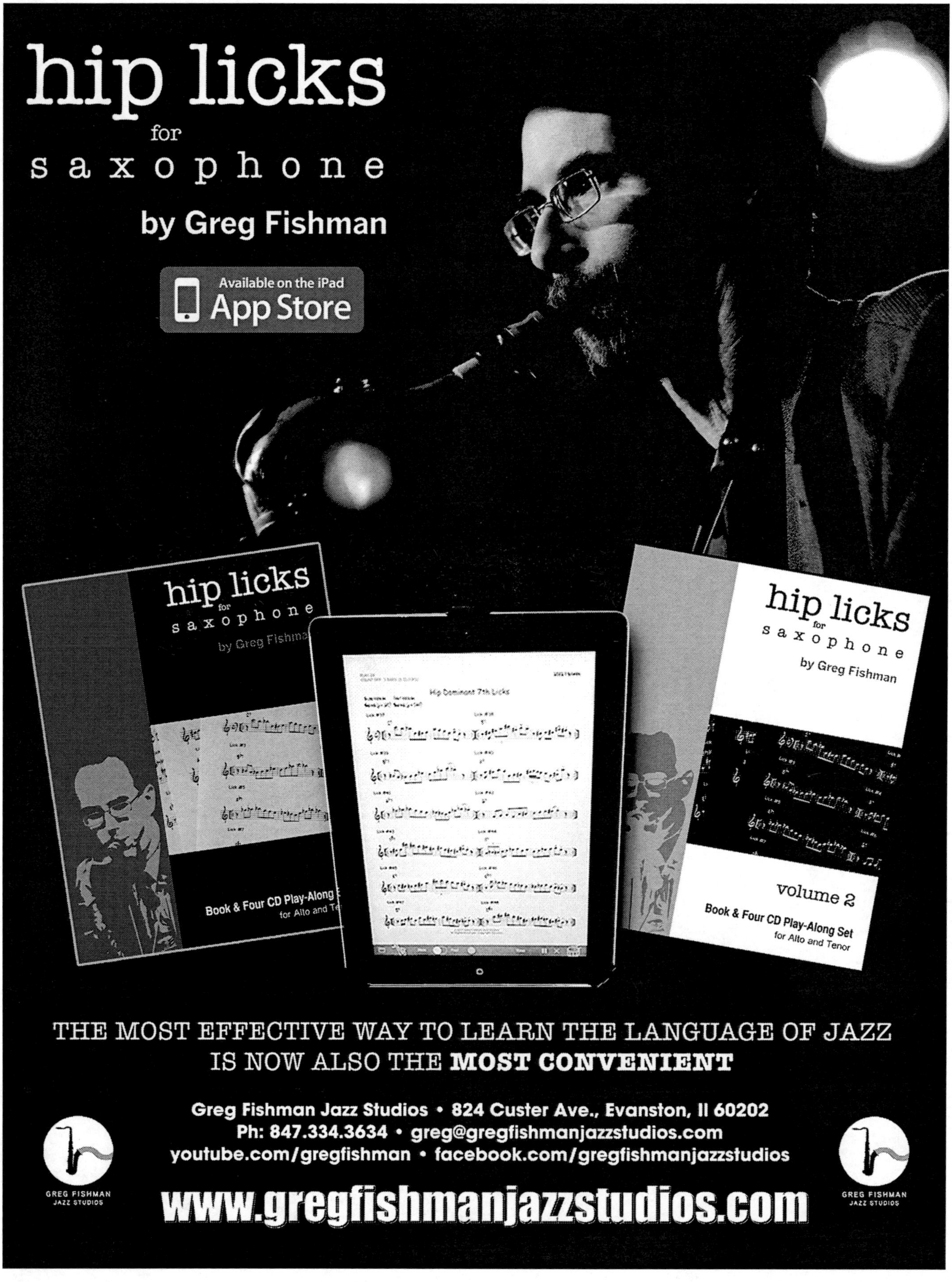
hip licks
for
saxophone
by Greg Fishman
Available on the iPad
App Store
hip licks
for
saxophone
by Greg Fishman
volume 2
Book & Four CD Play-Along Set
for Alto and Tenor
THE MOST EFFECTIVE WAY TO LEARN THE LANGUAGE OF JAZZ
IS NOW ALSO THE MOST CONVENIENT
Greg Fishman Jazz Studios • 824 Custer Ave., Evanston, Il 60202
Ph: 847.334.3634 • greg@gregfishmanjazzstudios.com
youtube.com/gregfishman • facebook.com/gregfishmanjazzstudios
GREG FISHMAN JAZZ STUDIOS
www.gregfishmanjazzstudios.com
GREG FISHMAN JAZZ STUDIOS

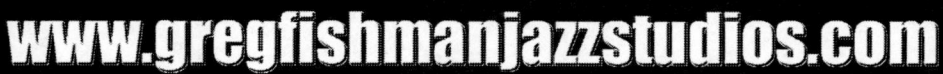

The new book by *Hip Licks* author Greg Fishman, illustrated by New Yorker cartoonist Mick Stevens, with foreword by Jeff Coffin.

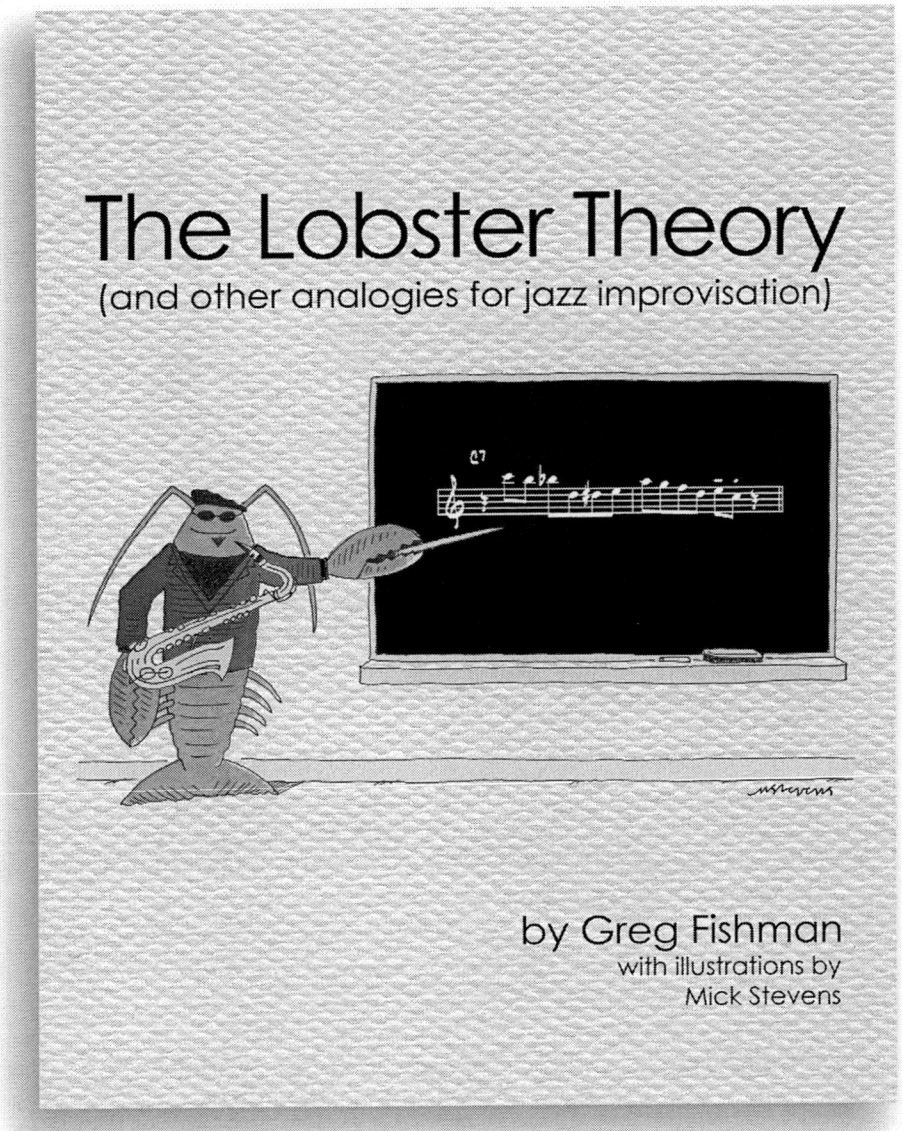

The Lobster Theory is a groundbreaking new approach to learning the language of jazz. It's a book of musical concepts brought to life through the use of analogies and illustrations.

"What Greg Fishman has accomplished in this book is to explain, and then show – through the use of awesome drawings and complete musical examples – different concepts and ideas that are essential to our development as musicians. **The Lobster Theory** is a really fun read and I enjoy Greg's sense of humor and wit. The ideas he presents here are effective, long lasting and inviting for students and educators alike."

– **Jeff Coffin**

See samples from the new book at:
www.gregfishmanjazzstudios.com

About the Author

Saxophonist and flutist Greg Fishman is an accomplished performer, recording artist, author, teacher and clinician. Born in Chicago in 1967, he began playing professionally at age fourteen. Greg graduated from DePaul University in Chicago with a degree in Jazz Performance, and earned a Masters Degree in Jazz Pedagogy from Northwestern University. He is among the foremost experts on the music of Stan Getz and is the author of three Getz transcription books published by Hal Leonard. His self-published books, *Jazz Saxophone Etudes, Volumes 1 – 3, Jazz Saxophone Duets, Volumes 1 – 3, Jazz Phrasing for Saxophone, Volumes 1 – 3, Hip Licks for Saxophone, Volumes 1 – 2, Jazz Guitar Etudes, Jazz Trumpet Duets, Hip Licks for Trumpet, Tasting Harmony™* and *The Lobster Theory* are in circulation worldwide and have been endorsed by top educators and jazz performers, including Michael Brecker, Jerry Coker, Bob Sheppard, James Moody and Phil Woods.

Greg is a contributing author of jazz theory articles for Jazz Improv magazine, JAZZed, Chicago Jazz Magazine, IAJE Jazz Educators Journal, and was featured on the cover of *Saxophone Journal*, for whom he also writes. He is the author of the liner notes for the Verve reissue of the Getz recording *The Steamer*.

Greg has toured and performed worldwide with his own group, and with such artists as the Woody Herman Band, Louis Bellson, Slide Hampton, Conte Candoli, Lou Levy, Clark Terry, Jackie and Roy, Don Menza, Ira Sullivan, Judy Roberts, Jeremy Monteiro, Jimmy Heath, Lou Donaldson, Harry Allen, Jeff Hamilton, Eddie Higgins, and Benny Golson.

In addition to clubs and concerts in the U.S., Greg has been featured at the Concord-Fujitsu jazz festival in Japan, the NorthSea Jazz Festival in the Netherlands, and in numerous concerts in Hong Kong, Bangkok, Singapore, China and Israel.

Greg teaches jazz master classes and college workshops nationally and internationally, and is on the faculty of the Jamey Aebersold Summer Jazz Workshop.

When not on tour, Greg is based in the Chicago area where he performs locally and teaches at Greg Fishman Jazz Studios.

Greg Fishman is a D'Addario Woodwind artist and plays Rico reeds exclusively.

"...His solos are shrewdly conceived yet delivered with apparent ease and elegance. He develops harmonies that sometimes startle the ear as he forges lines that take unexpected twists and turns..."
— Chicago Tribune

"Greg Fishman dares to explore new musical heights. Every lesson in Greg's books is a must for all musicians, and this latest book is no exception. Greg, you've done a beautiful, musical thing again!"
— James Moody